INCORPORATED 1868

CATALOGUE NUMBER 31

OF THE

VISES

Grindstone Frames, Machinists'
Tools and Other
Specialties

MADE BY

Athol Machine Company

Athol, Mass., U. S. A.

CABLE ADDRESS—CHOPPERS, ATHOL

CODES—ATLANTIC CABLE, WESTERN UNION

ATHOL MACHINE CO.   ATHOL, MASS. U.S.A.

Please Note

Our goods are made by skilled mechanics and are carefully inspected. We agree to replace anything found to be defective in material or construction.

For special warranty in regard to Vises, see page 80.

When goods are returned for repairs or for other reason, the name of the sender must be plainly marked on the package, and the transportation charges prepaid. A letter giving full information as to what is wanted should be mailed at the time goods are sent.

Mechanics and manufacturers are requested to order our goods through hardware dealers. In places in the United States and Canada where the trade do not sell our goods, we will send them prepaid on receipt of prices given in this Catalogue.

Dealers without adequate commercial rating, desiring credit, must furnish satisfactory references.

Goods will not be sent C. O. D. unless the order is accompanied by a sufficient amount to pay transportation charges both ways.

Our goods are sold to dealers f. o. b. here, at purchaser's risk after shipment.

Customers are requested to give specific shipping directions with each order. In the absence of such instruction we shall ship, at purchaser's risk, by what we consider the best way, safety, quickness, and cheapness being considered.

If desired, we can join our shipments with goods being sent by **The L. S. Starrett Co.** of this place.

Please destroy previous Catalogues and order only from this edition, No. 31.

Order by number, to save time and mistakes.

Vise Display Stands

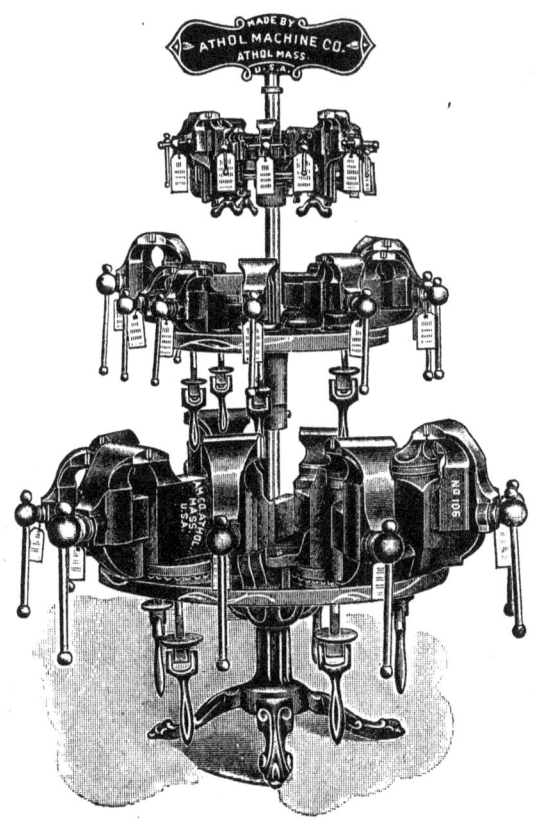

ATHOL MACHINE CO.　　　　　　ATHOL, MASS. U.S.A.

To Sell Vises

Don't keep them in a corner down cellar; put them where people will see them.

The illustration on the preceding page shows a stand which we are supplying to the trade for the display of our vises. These stands are not sold but loaned. They remain the property of the Athol Machine Co. and are to be used only for displaying Athol Machine Co. vises. They are sent only in connection with an order for vises as per a list which will be sent to dealers on application, or equivalent in value.

Any other of our vises having the same width of jaw may be substituted for the numbers given in schedule, the list and net price, of course, changing according to the vises selected. In case we do not have a certain size of vise in stock we will substitute in order to avoid delay in shipment. This will make a slight variation in price.

To set up display stand slide the shelves and collars on to the standard before placing same into base. The name plate is not intended to be taken from the standard. Place the collar underneath the second shelf $10\frac{1}{2}$ in. from the top of lower shelf. Screw up set screw tightly to the standard where spotted. Set the collar underneath shelf and set up set screw as before. Place the vises commencing with the first on the list on each shelf going to the right, and the vises will fit on as illustrated and as specified in list.

Height of stand, 57 in. Extreme diameter, with vises, 45 in. For domestic shipment the stand is crated all set up; net weight 125 lbs., gross 143 lbs. For ocean shipment it is knocked down and boxed; net 125 lbs., gross 200 lbs.

ATHOL MACHINE CO. ATHOL, MASS. U.S.A.

The Simpson Patent Adjustable Parallel Vise

The Simplest and the Best quick-adjusting Vise in the world

This Vise is operated in the same manner as an ordinary screw vise, or it can be instantly opened or closed the full length, by a single movement of the hand, without the use of the screw, the screw being used merely to give the grip after adjusting the jaws to the work; thus combining a quick adjustment with all the advantages of the best screw vise—points not found combined in any other vise made.

By slightly raising the front jaw the screw and nut are disengaged; the jaw can then be moved in or out as may be required to adjust it to its work, and on removing the hand it instantly drops into place, the screw and nut again become engaged, and a single turn of the screw gives the required grip.

These vises are scientifically proportioned for the greatest strength and durability, as well as convenience in use, and there is no complicated mechanism, as in other quick-adjusting vises, to be constantly getting out of repair. Their extreme simplicity is one of their strongest features.

Note the completeness of this line, the sizes running from $1\frac{1}{8}$ in. to 5 in.

The constant and rapidly increasing demand for these vises is the best evidence of their superiority.

Every vise is fully warranted, and if one fails in any particular, by any reasonable usage, it will be replaced **free of charge or the money refunded.** See page 80.

ATHOL MACHINE CO. ATHOL, MASS. U.S.A.

0
1
2
10

The Simpson Vise

Quick Acting

Jewelers' and Artisans' Clamp Vise

With smooth-faced, tempered steel jaws

Fully warranted—see page 80

	Width of Jaws	Jaws open	Weight	Price
No. 0	$1\frac{1}{5}$ in.	$1\frac{1}{4}$ in.	$1\frac{1}{2}$ lbs.	$1.25
No. 1	$1\frac{5}{8}$ "	$1\frac{3}{4}$ "	$2\frac{3}{4}$ "	1.75
No. 2	$2\frac{1}{8}$ "	2 "	$5\frac{3}{4}$ "	2.75

Jewelers' and Artisans' Swivel Vise

With smooth-faced, tempered steel jaws

Fully warranted—see page 80

	Width of Jaws	Jaws open	Weight	Price
No. 10	$2\frac{3}{8}$ in.	2 in.	$6\frac{1}{4}$ lbs.	$3.50

11 12 13 14 15 16

The Simpson Vise

Quick Acting

With check or smooth-faced, tempered steel jaws

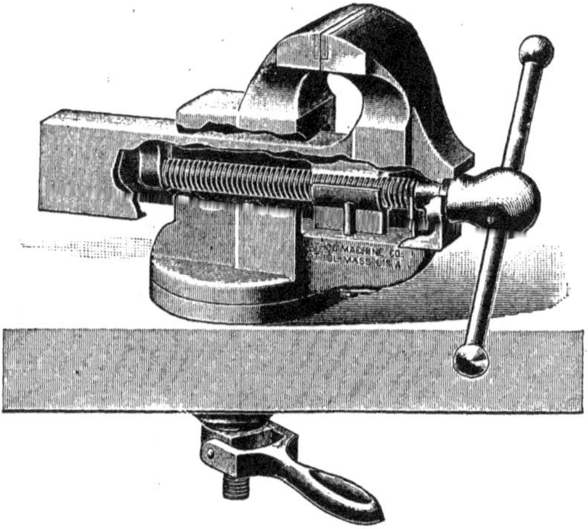

Machinists' Swivel Base Bench Vise

Nos. 12, 13, 14, and 15 will be furnished with smooth jaws when so ordered, at no extra cost.

Nos. 11 and 16 have checked jaws.

Fully warranted—see page 80

	Width of Jaws	Jaws open	Weight	Price
No. 11	2½ in.	2¾ in.	9½ lbs.	$5.00
No. 12	3 "	3¼ "	17½ "	7.00
No. 13	3½ "	4 "	28 "	8.75
No. 14	4 "	5 "	44 "	10.50
No. 15	4½ "	5¾ "	59 "	12.50
No. 16	5 "	6¼ "	78 "	16.00

ATHOL MACHINE CO. ATHOL, MASS. U.S.A.

The Simpson Vise

Quick Acting

With check or smooth-faced, tempered steel jaws

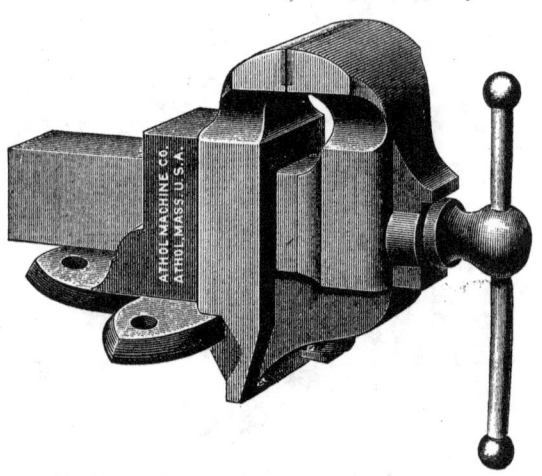

Machinists' Stationary Base Bench Vise

No. 27 has smooth-faced, tempered steel jaws.
Nos. 29, 30, 31, and 32 will be furnished with smooth jaws when so ordered, at no extra cost.
Nos. 28 and 33 have checked jaws.

Fully warranted—see page 80

	Width of Jaws	Jaws open	Weight	Price
No. 27	$2\frac{1}{8}$ in.	2 in.	$5\frac{1}{2}$ lbs.	$3.25
No. 28	$2\frac{1}{2}$ "	$2\frac{3}{4}$ "	9 "	4.25
No. 29	3 "	$3\frac{1}{4}$ "	$15\frac{1}{2}$ "	5.50
No. 30	$3\frac{1}{2}$ "	4 "	26 "	7.00
No. 31	4 "	5 "	37 "	8.50
No. 32	$4\frac{1}{2}$ "	$5\frac{3}{4}$ "	49 "	10.00
No. 33	5 "	$6\frac{1}{2}$ "	64 "	13.00

The Simpson Vise

Quick Acting

With check-faced, tempered steel jaws

Machinists' Stationary Base, Swivel Jaw Bench Vise

The Swivel Jaw Vise will adapt itself to an angular piece of work, as shown in illustrations, and is invaluable to a factory equipment.

Fully warranted—see page 80

	Width of Jaws	Jaws open	Weight	Price
No. 107	3½ in.	4 in.	32 lbs.	$8.50
No. 109	4 "	5 "	46 "	10.50
No. 111	4½ "	6 "	64 "	13.00

ATHOL MACHINE CO.   ATHOL, MASS. U.S.A.

108
110
112

The Simpson Vise

Quick Acting

With check-faced, tempered steel jaws

Machinists' Swivel Base, Swivel Jaw Bench Vise

Fully warranted—see page 80

	Width of Jaws	Jaws open	Weight	Price
No. 108	3½ in.	4 in.	34 lbs.	$9.50
No. 110	4 "	5 "	53 "	12.50
No. 112	4⅛ "	6 "	74 "	16.00

ATHOL MACHINE CO. ATHOL, MASS. U.S.A.

The Simpson Vise

Quick Acting

With smooth-faced, tempered steel jaws

Stationary Base, Coachmakers', Carpenters', and Pattern Workers' Bench Vise

Fully warranted—see page 80

	Width of Jaws	Jaws open	Weight	Price
No. 40	4 in.	8½ in.	41 lbs.	$9.00
No. 41	4½ "	10½ "	49 "	10.00

ATHOL MACHINE CO. ATHOL, MASS. U.S.A.

42

43

The Simpson Vise

Quick Acting

With smooth-faced, tempered steel jaws

Swivel Base, Coachmakers', Carpenters', and Pattern Workers' Bench Vise

Fully warranted—see page 80

	Width of Jaws	Jaws open	Weight	Price
No. 42	4 in.	8½ in.	48 lbs.	$11.00
No. 43	4¼ "	10¼ "	58 "	12.00

ATHOL MACHINE CO. ATHOL, MASS. U.S.A.

44
45

The Simpson Vise

Quick Acting

With smooth-faced, tempered steel jaws

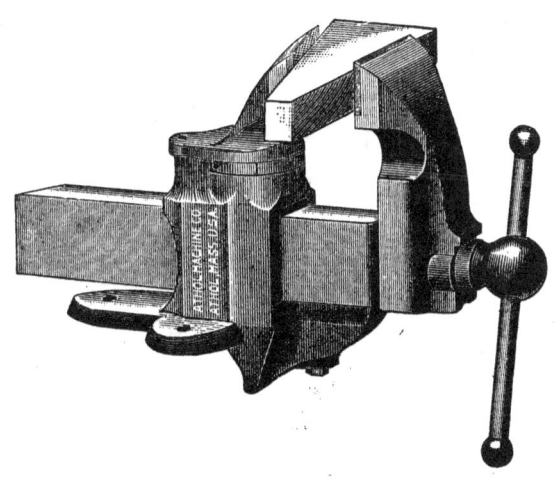

Stationary Base, Swivel Jaw, Coachmakers', Carpenters', and Pattern Workers' Bench Vise

For workmanship and finish, as well as for strength and durability, we challenge comparison with any vise made.

Fully warranted—see page 80

	Width of Jaws	Jaws open	Weight	Price
No. 44	4 in.	8½ in.	43 lbs.	$11.50
No. 45	4½ "	10¼ "	51 "	12.50

ATHOL MACHINE CO.   ATHOL, MASS. U.S.A.

46

47

The Simpson Vise

Quick Acting

With smooth-faced, tempered steel jaws

Swivel Base, Swivel Jaw, Coachmakers', Carpenters', and Pattern Workers' Bench Vise

For carriage and agricultural implement makers, or any class of woodworkers who require an iron vise, these vises are absolutely unapproached.

Fully warranted—see page 80

	Width of Jaws	Jaws open	Weight	Price
No. 46	4 in.	8½ in.	52 lbs.	$13.00
No. 47	4½ "	10¼ "	62 "	14.00

ATHOL MACHINE CO. ATHOL, MASS. U.S.A.

50
51
60
62

Amateur Vises

With smooth-faced, tempered steel jaws

Fully warranted — see page 80

Nos. 60 and 62 have steel jaws and wrought iron screws, and No. 62 has a steel swivel jaw attachment as shown in cut.

	Width of Jaws	Jaws open	Weight	Price
No. 60	1½ in.	1¾ in.	1¾ lbs.	$0.50
No. 62	2 "	2¼ "	3¼ "	1.00

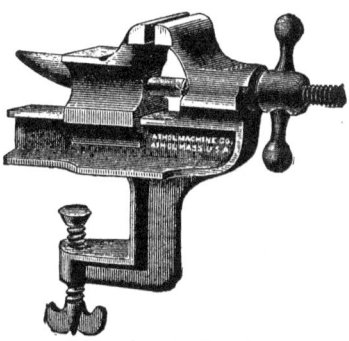

With smooth-faced jaws

The best Vise made for the money

	Width of Jaws	Jaws open	Weight	Price
No. 50	1½ in.	1⅓ in.	1⅓ lbs.	0.25
No. 51	2 "	1¾ "	2¼ "	.35

ATHOL MACHINE CO.   ATHOL, MASS. U.S.A.

3
4
5

Standard Vise

Jewelers' and Artisans' Clamp Vise

With smooth-faced, tempered steel jaws

Vise No. 5 is admirably adapted to attach to the running board of an automobile or seat of a motor boat for a quick repair. This applies also to No. 2, page 6.

Note completeness of our line, the sizes running from $1\frac{1}{8}$ in. to 7 in. (page 18).

Fully warranted—see page 80

	Width of Jaws	Jaws open	Weight	Price
No. 3	$1\frac{1}{8}$ in.	$1\frac{1}{4}$ in.	$1\frac{1}{2}$ lbs.	$1.40
No. 4	$1\frac{5}{8}$ "	$1\frac{3}{4}$ "	$2\frac{3}{4}$ "	2.00
No. 5	$2\frac{1}{8}$ "	2 "	$5\frac{3}{4}$ "	3.15

ATHOL MACHINE CO.   ATHOL, MASS. U.S.A.

Standard Vise

With check or smooth-faced, tempered steel jaws

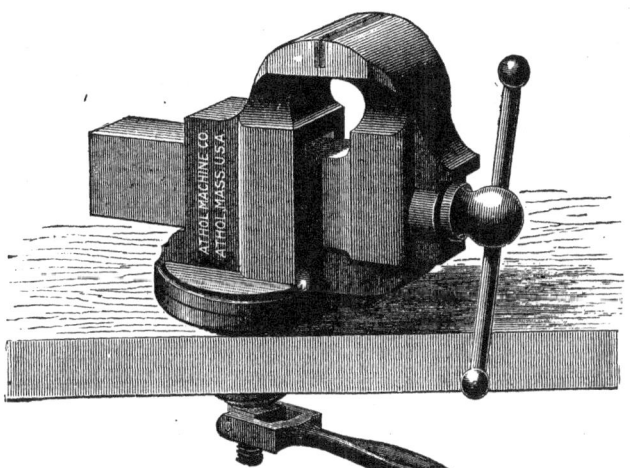

Machinists' Swivel Base Bench Vise

These vises are the same in all respects as the Simpson Vise, with the exception of the quick adjustment, and are unquestionably the best solid nut screw vises made for machinists' use.

No. 77 has smooth-faced, tempered steel jaws.

Nos. 79, 80, 81, and 82 will be furnished with smooth jaws when so ordered, at no extra cost.

Nos. 78 and 83 have checked jaws.

Fully warranted—see page 80

	Width of Jaws	Jaws open	Weight	Price
No. 77	2¼ in.	2 in.	6¼ lbs.	$3.50
No. 78	2½ "	2¾ "	9½ "	5.00
No. 79	3 "	3¼ "	18 "	7.00
No. 80	3½ "	4 "	28½ "	8.75
No. 81	4 "	5 "	45 "	10.50
No. 82	4½ "	6 "	60 "	12.50
No. 83	5 "	7 "	80 "	16.00

ATHOL MACHINE CO.　　　　　ATHOL, MASS. U.S.A.

87
88
89
90
91
92
93
94
95
96

Standard Vise

With check or smooth-faced, tempered steel jaws

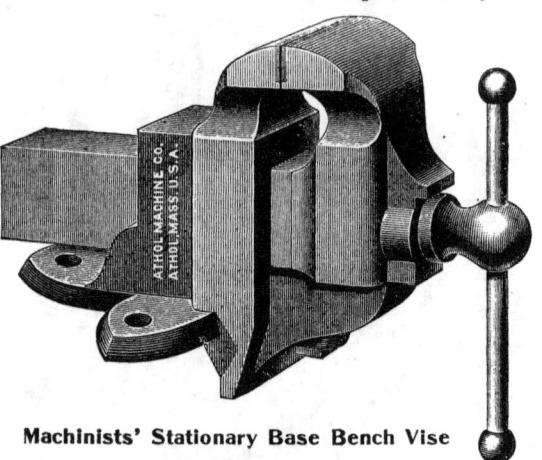

Machinists' Stationary Base Bench Vise

No. 87 has smooth-faced, tempered steel jaws.
Nos. 89, 90, 91, and 92 will be furnished with smooth jaws when so ordered, at no extra cost.
Nos. 88, 93, 94, 95, and 96 have checked jaws.

Fully warranted—see page 80

	Width of Jaws	Jaws open	Weight	Price
No. 87	2⅛ in.	2 in.	5½ lbs.	$3.25
No. 88	2½ "	2¾ "	9 "	4.25
No. 89	3 "	3½ "	16 "	5.50
No. 90	3½ "	4 "	26½ "	7.00
No. 91	4 "	5 "	38 "	8.50
No. 92	4½ "	6 "	50 "	10.00
No. 93	5 "	7 "	65 "	13.00

Stationary Base, Extra Heavy Chipping Vise

	Width of Jaws	Jaws open	Weight	Price
No. 94	5½ in.	8 in.	100 lbs.	$18.50
No. 95	6 "	9 "	135 "	25.00
No. 96	7 "	10½ "	190 "	30.00

ATHOL MACHINE CO.   ATHOL, MASS. U.S.A.

Standard Vise

With check or smooth-faced, tempered steel jaws

**77
78
79
80
81
82
83**

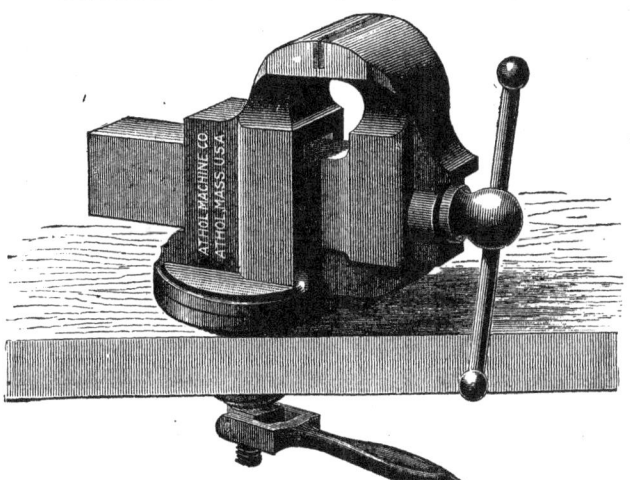

Machinists' Swivel Base Bench Vise

These vises are the same in all respects as the Simpson Vise, with the exception of the quick adjustment, and are unquestionably the best solid nut screw vises made for machinists' use.

No. 77 has smooth-faced, tempered steel jaws.

Nos. 79, 80, 81, and 82 will be furnished with smooth jaws when so ordered, at no extra cost.

Nos. 78 and 83 have checked jaws.

Fully warranted—see page 80

	Width of Jaws	Jaws open	Weight	Price
No. 77	$2\frac{1}{4}$ in.	2 in.	$6\frac{1}{4}$ lbs.	$3.50
No. 78	$2\frac{1}{2}$ "	$2\frac{3}{4}$ "	$9\frac{1}{2}$ "	5.00
No. 79	3 "	$3\frac{1}{4}$ "	18 "	7.00
No. 80	$3\frac{1}{2}$ "	4 "	$28\frac{1}{2}$ "	8.75
No. 81	4 "	5 "	45 "	10.50
No. 82	$4\frac{1}{2}$ "	6 "	60 "	12.50
No. 83	5 "	7 "	80 "	16.00

ATHOL MACHINE CO.   ATHOL, MASS. U.S.A.

87
88
89
90
91
92
93
94
95
96

Standard Vise

With check or smooth-faced, tempered steel jaws

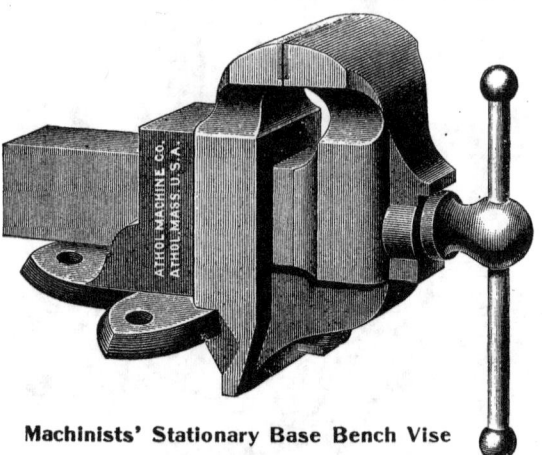

Machinists' Stationary Base Bench Vise

No. 87 has smooth-faced, tempered steel jaws.
Nos. 89, 90, 91, and 92 will be furnished with smooth jaws when so ordered, at no extra cost.
Nos. 88, 93, 94, 95, and 96 have checked jaws.

Fully warranted—see page 80

	Width of Jaws	Jaws open	Weight	Price
No. 87	2¼ in.	2 in.	5½ lbs.	$3.25
No. 88	2½ "	2¾ "	9 "	4.25
No. 89	3 "	3½ "	16 "	5.50
No. 90	3½ "	4 "	26½ "	7.00
No. 91	4 "	5 "	38 "	8.50
No. 92	4½ "	6 "	50 "	10.00
No. 93	5 "	7 "	65 "	13.00

Stationary Base, Extra Heavy Chipping Vise

	Width of Jaws	Jaws open	Weight	Price
No. 94	5½ in.	8 in.	100 lbs.	$18.50
No. 95	6 "	9 "	135 "	25.00
No. 96	7 "	10½ "	190 "	30.00

ATHOL MACHINE CO.   ATHOL, MASS. U.S.A.

101
Standard Vise
103
105

With check-faced, tempered steel jaws

Machinists' Stationary Base, Swivel Jaw Bench Vise

Fully warranted—see page 80

	Width of Jaws	Jaws open	Weight	Price
No. 101	$3\frac{1}{2}$ in.	4 in.	32 lbs.	$8.50
No. 103	4 "	5 "	46 "	10.50
No. 105	$4\frac{1}{2}$ "	6 "	64 "	13.00

ATHOL MACHINE CO. ATHOL, MASS. U.S.A.

102
104
106

Standard Vise

With check-faced, tempered steel jaws

Machinists' Swivel Base, Swivel Jaw Bench Vise

Fully warranted—see page 80

	Width of Jaws	Jaws open	Weight	Price
No. 102	3½ in.	4 in.	34 lbs.	$9.50
No. 104	4 "	5 "	53 "	12.50
No. 106	4½ "	6 "	74 "	16.00

ATHOL MACHINE CO.　　　ATHOL, MASS. U.S.A.

Standard Vise

101
103
105

With check-faced, tempered steel jaws

Machinists' Stationary Base, Swivel Jaw Bench Vise

Fully warranted—see page 80

	Width of Jaws	Jaws open	Weight	Price
No. 101	3½ in.	4 in.	32 lbs.	$8.50
No. 103	4 "	5 "	46 "	10.50
No. 105	4¼ "	6 "	64 "	13.00

ATHOL MACHINE CO.   ATHOL, MASS. U.S.A.

102
104
106

Standard Vise

With check-faced, tempered steel jaws

Machinists' Swivel Base, Swivel Jaw Bench Vise

Fully warranted—see page 80

	Width of Jaws	Jaws open	Weight	Price
No. 102	3½ in.	4 in.	34 lbs.	$9.50
No. 104	4 "	5 "	53 "	12.50
No. 106	4½ "	6 "	74 "	16.00

20

ATHOL MACHINE CO.   ATHOL, MASS. U.S.A.

Oval Slide Vise

With check-faced, tempered steel jaws

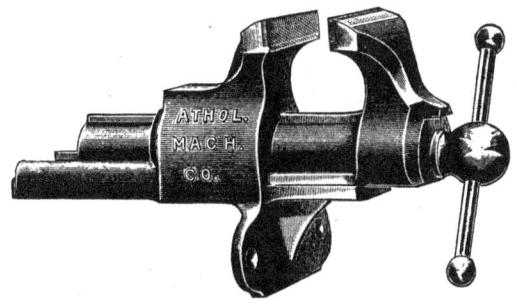

Made of best quality of stock and proportioned for strength and durability.

Fully warranted—see page 80

	Width of Jaws	Jaws open	Weight	Price
No. 63	2 in.	3 in.	7 lbs.	$1.70
No. 64	$2\frac{1}{2}$ "	$3\frac{1}{4}$ "	$7\frac{1}{2}$ "	2.20
No. 65	3 "	$4\frac{1}{2}$ "	$16\frac{1}{2}$ "	3.00
No. 66	$3\frac{1}{2}$ "	$5\frac{3}{4}$ "	27 "	3.80
No. 67	4 "	$6\frac{1}{4}$ "	36 "	5.00

ATHOL MACHINE CO.   ATHOL, MASS. U.S.A.

69
70
71
72

Farmers' Vises

With check-faced, tempered steel jaws

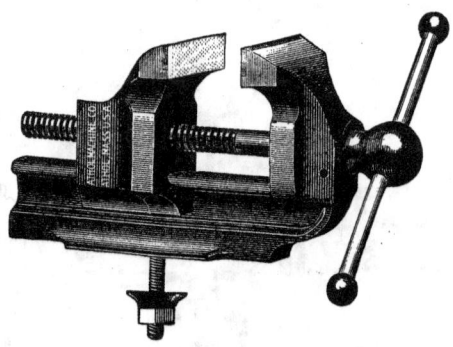

These vises are designed to meet the large and growing demand among farmers and others for a cheap, strong vise.

They are made from the best of material, and are proportioned for the greatest possible strength for the size of the vise, while in workmanship and finish they are not surpassed by any of the high-priced vises.

Fully warranted—see page 80

	Width of Jaws	Jaws open	Weight	Price
No. 69	3 in.	3 in.	8 lbs.	$1.75
No. 70	3½ "	4 "	12 "	2.25
No. 71	4 "	5 "	22 "	3.50
No. 72	4½ "	6 "	34 "	5.00

ATHOL MACHINE CO. ATHOL, MASS. U.S.A.

Standard Pipe Grip
No. 150

		Price
No. 150 A.	Fits any 3 to 4¾ in. Machinist's Vise, Will hold ¼ to 2½ in. pipe.	$2.50
No. 150 B.	Fits any 5 to 6½ in. Machinist's Vise, Will hold ¼ to 5 in. pipe.	2.75
No. 150 C.	Fits any 7 to 8½ in. Machinist's Vise, Will hold ¼ to 6 in. pipe.	3.00

Extra Parts for Vises

In ordering Extra Parts for vises, give number of vise and width of jaw, and, if for Standard Vise, state if the front jaw has the number 1894 cast on one side.

It is absolutely necessary that we have these particulars in order to send jaws that will fit.

Do not send us a broken vise jaw, and request us to send another like it. We make several vises of the same size, the jaws of which will not interchange, and we cannot always tell from broken parts what to send.

If the *unbroken* jaw is sent us, and the number of the vise given, we will fit a new jaw, and no charge will be made for fitting.

See next page for prices

ATHOL MACHINE CO. ATHOL, MASS. U.S.A.

Prices of Extra Parts of Vises

No.	Back Jaw	Front Jaw	Nut	Screw and Handle	Wrench	Bench Screw	Washer	Swivel Plate	Swivel Jaw	Swivel Jaw Nut
0	$0.50	$0.50	$0.25	$0.20	....	....	....	....	....	....
1	.65	.65	.25	.35	....	....	....	....	....	....
2	1.00	1.00	.25	.60	....	....	....	....	....	....
3	.50	.50	.25	.20	....	....	....	....	....	....
4	.65	.65	.25	.35	....	....	....	....	....	....
5	1.00	1.00	.25	.60	....	....	....	....	....	....
10	1.25	1.25	.25	.60	$0.15	$0.10	$0.10	$0.15	....	....
11	1.75	1.75	.35	.80	.25	.10	.10	.15	....	....
12	2.50	2.75	.35	1.00	.30	.10	.10	.20	....	....
13	3.00	3.50	.40	1.25	.35	.15	.10	.30	....	....
14	3.75	4.00	.45	1.50	.40	.15	.15	.40	....	....
15	4.75	5.00	.50	1.75	.45	.20	.15	.50	....	....
16	6.00	6.50	.60	2.00	.45	.20	.15	.70	....	....
27	1.25	1.25	.25	.60	....	....	....	....	....	....
28	1.75	1.75	.35	.80	....	....	....	....	....	....
29	2.50	2.75	.35	1.00	....	....	....	....	....	....
30	3.00	3.50	.40	1.25	....	....	....	....	....	....
31	3.75	4.00	.45	1.50	....	....	....	....	....	....
32	4.00	4.75	.50	1.75	....	....	....	....	....	....
33	5.00	5.50	.60	2.00	....	....	....	....	....	....
40	4.00	4.50	.45	1.75	....	....	....	....	....	....
41	4.50	5.00	.50	2.00	....	....	....	....	....	....
42	4.25	4.50	.45	1.75	.40	.15	.15	.40	....	....
43	4.75	5.00	.50	2.00	.50	.20	.15	.50	....	....
44	5.40	4.50	.45	1.75	....	....	....	....	$2.25	$0.50
45	5.90	5.00	.50	1.75	....	....	....	....	2.50	.60
46	5.75	4.50	.45	1.75	.40	.15	.15	.40	2.25	.50
47	6.25	5.00	.50	1.75	.40	.15	.15	.40	2.50	.60
50	.10	.15	.10	....	....	....	....	....	....	....
51	.15	.25	.10	....	....	....	....	....	....	....
60	.15	.25	....	.20	....	....	....	....	....	....
62	.30	.50	....	.40	....	....	....	....	....	....
63	.90	.90	.35	.60	....	....	....	....	....	....
64	1.00	1.00	.35	.60	....	....	....	....	....	....
65	1.35	1.15	.40	1.00	....	....	....	....	....	....

ATHOL MACHINE CO. ATHOL, MASS. U.S.A.

Extra Vise Parts (Continued)

No.	Back Jaw	Front Jaw	Nut	Screw and Handle	Wrench	Bench Screw	Washer	Swivel Plate	Swivel Jaw	Swivel Jaw Nut
66	$1.75	$1.50	$0.50	$1.25	....	....	....	....	....	....
67	2.50	2.00	.60	2.00	....	....	....	....	....	....
69	.50	.65	.20	.60	....	$0.10	....	....	....	....
70	.75	1.10	.20	.75	....	.10	....	....	....	....
71	1.10	1.85	.20	1.00	....	.15	....	....	....	....
72	1.75	2.80	.25	1.25	....	.15	....	....	....	....
77	1.25	1.25	.25	.60	$0.15	.10	$0.10	$0.15	....	....
78	1.75	1.75	.35	.80	.25	.10	.10	.15	....	....
79	2.50	2.75	.35	1.00	.30	.10	.10	.20	....	....
80	3.00	3.50	.40	1.25	.35	.15	.10	.30	....	....
81	3.75	4.00	.45	1.50	.40	.15	.15	.40	....	....
82	4.75	5.00	.50	1.75	.45	.20	.15	.50	....	....
83	6.00	6.50	.60	2.00	.45	.20	.15	.70	....	....
87	1.25	1.25	.25	.60	....	....	....	....	....	....
88	1.75	1.75	.35	.80	....	....	....	....	....	....
89	2.50	2.75	.35	1.00	....	....	....	....	....	....
90	3.00	3.50	.40	1.25	....	....	....	....	....	....
91	3.75	4.00	.45	1.50	....	....	....	....	....	....
92	4.00	4.75	.50	1.75	....	....	....	....	....	....
93	5.00	5.50	.60	2.00	....	....	....	....	....	....
94	7.00	8.00	1.00	3.00	....	....	....	....	....	....
95	9.00	10.00	1.25	4.00	....	....	....	....	....	....
96	11.50	12.50	1.50	5.00	....	....	....	....	....	....
101	4.25	3.50	.40	1.25	....	....	....	....	$2.00	$0.40
102	4.25	3.50	.40	1.25	.35	.15	.10	.30	2.00	.40
103	5.70	4.00	.45	1.50	....	....	....	....	2.25	.50
104	5.70	4.00	.45	1.50	.40	.15	.15	.40	2.25	.50
105	7.25	5.00	.50	1.75	....	....	....	....	2.50	.60
106	7.75	5.00	.50	1.75	.45	.20	.15	.50	2.50	.60
107	4.25	3.50	.40	1.25	....	....	....	....	2.00	.40
108	4.25	3.50	.40	1.25	.35	.15	.10	.30	2.00	.40
109	5.70	4.00	.45	1.50	....	....	....	....	2.25	.50
110	5.70	4.00	.45	1.50	.40	.15	.15	.40	2.25	.50
111	7.25	5.00	.50	1.75	....	....	....	....	2.50	.60
112	7.75	5.00	.50	1.75	.45	.20	.15	.50	2.50	.60

Household Grindstone

No. **154**

This Grindstone is admirably adapted for grinding small tools used by jewelers, amateur mechanics, etc., as well as for hotel or household purposes. The frame is strong and well made. The stone, 14 in. x 1¾ in., is carefully selected of the proper grit to do the work intended. Weight, 60 pounds.

Price, each $4.50

ATHOL MACHINE CO.   ATHOL, MASS. U.S.A.

Iron Grindstone Frame
No. 155

With adjustable tool rest, and truing attachment

Weight, ready for shipment, 500 pounds
Pulley, 20 in. diameter, 5 in. face
Boxes Babbitt lined
Takes stone 42 in. diameter, 6 in. face
Price complete, without stone $50.00
Price with stone quoted on request

ATHOL MACHINE CO.　　　ATHOL, MASS. U.S.A.

Iron Grindstone Frame No. 156

With water guard and adjustable tool rest

Takes stone 30 in. diameter and 4 in. face
Boxes Babbitt lined
Weight ready for shipment, 170 pounds

PRICES

Frame as illustrated	$15.00
Plain frame, without pulley or treadle attachment	12.00
Pulley, 15 in. diameter, 3 in. face	1.50
Treadle	1.50

Pulley has removable handle attached, as shown in cut
Price with stone quoted on request

Iron Grindstone Frame

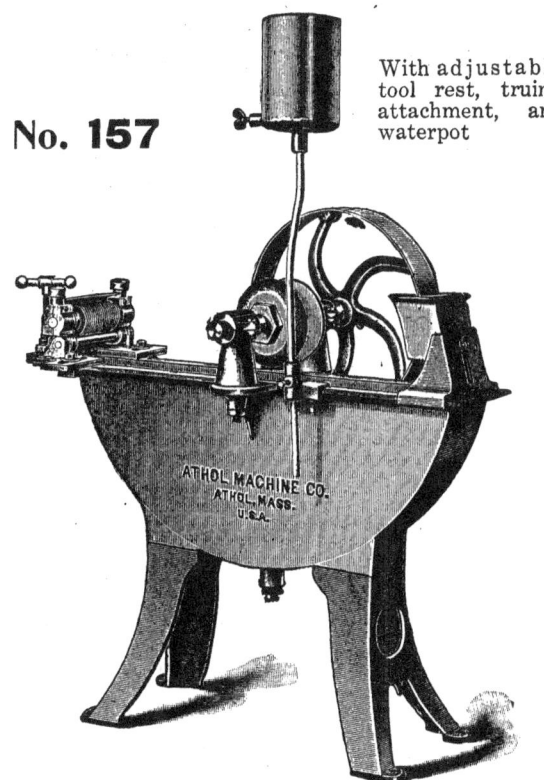

No. 157

With adjustable tool rest, truing attachment, and waterpot

Takes stone 30 in. diameter and 4 in. face
Boxes Babbitt lined
Weight ready for shipment, 175 pounds
Price complete, as illustrated $18.00
Without waterpot 17.00
Price with stone quoted on request

Adjustable Grindstone Truer
No. 161

Can be used on any iron frame with flange and not over 14½ in. wide. The efficiency and durability of a grindstone depend upon its being kept trued up on its face. You cannot afford to pay a mechanic to stand and true up a stone when you can buy this device for so little money. With this the constant attention of a man is not required. Turn down the adjusting screw, turn on the water, and the Truer does the rest. No dust flying all over the room. A perfect face on the stone all the time. No gouging the stone by a tool slipping from the workman's hand.

The steel cutters are set on the arbor at a sharp angle. The Truer leaves the stone with a straight, even face and the gritty surface necessary for good grinding.

PRICES

No. 161 A—Adjustable to fit frames from 6¼ in. to 10 in. wide, for stones of 2 in. to 4 in. face, length of cutting roll, 5 in. . $7.50
    Extra cutting roll 4.00

No. 161 B—Adjustable to fit frames from 9½ in. to 14½ in. wide, for stones of 4 in. to 6 in. face, length of cutting roll, 8 in. $15.00
    Extra cutting roll 7.50

ATHOL MACHINE CO. ATHOL, MASS. U.S.A.

Bench Grinder
No. 158

This is a neat, rigid, and practical grinder for bench use. As it occupies only a very small space, 9⅝ in. x 5 in. over all, height 7 in., a number of them may be located in different situations in a factory, thus effecting a considerable saving in workmen's time and especially when the slight cost of the grinders is considered.

This tool is indispensable for grinding drills, reamers, counterbores, and a hundred and one small tools as well as for rough grinding of small machine parts, castings, and forgings. All parts are painted or polished.

Size of base, 6 in. x 5 in. Length of spindle, 9⅝ in.
Height to center of spindle, 5⅜ in. Total height, 7 in.
Length of each bearing, 2¼ in. Diameter of spindle in bearing, ¾ in. Diameter of spindle for wheel, ½ in.
Distance between wheels, 6⅝ in. Diameter of flanges, 2¾ in. Width of pulley, 1⅜ in. Diameter of pulley, 2 in.
Size of emery wheels, 8 in. Nuts on spindle, case hardened, hexagon, 1 in.
Equipped with patent oil cups for bearings. Weight, 10 lbs.
For countershaft, see page 33. Each grinder neatly and securely packed for shipment.

Price, each, without emery wheels, $7.00

ATHOL MACHINE CO.   ATHOL, MASS. U.S.A.

Bench Grinder

No. 159

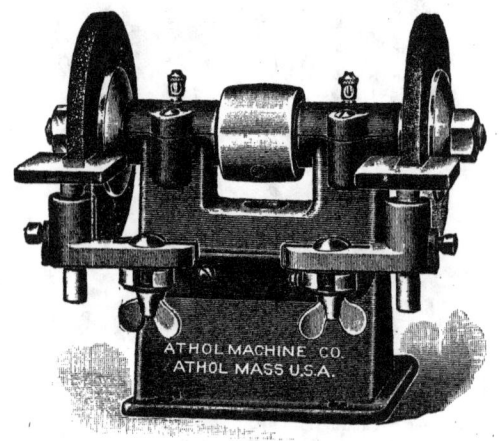

This grinder is identical with No. 158 on the preceding page, with the addition of adjustable rests, which can be used advantageously in grinding pieces alike, and may be quickly detached when not needed. Weight, 13 pounds. Each grinder neatly and securely packed for shipment.

For countershaft, see page 33.

Price, each, without emery wheels, $8.50

ATHOL MACHINE CO.   ATHOL, MASS. U.S.A.

Bench Grinder Countershaft
No. 160

The illustration obviates the need of verbal description. The belt is shipped by a simple turn of the lever. Fitted with drip cups to collect surplus oil.

Distance of drop to lower edge of drive pulley, 13½ in. Drive pulley, 12 in. x 2 in. Tight and loose pulley, 3½ in. x 1⅝ in. Diameter of shaft, ⅞ in. Length of shaft, 14 in. Weight, 26 lbs. Speed of counter, 530 revolutions.

Each countershaft neatly and securely packed for shipment.

Price, each, $8.00

ATHOL MACHINE CO.   ATHOL, MASS. U.S.A.

200
220 ## Premier Outside Spring Calipers No. 200

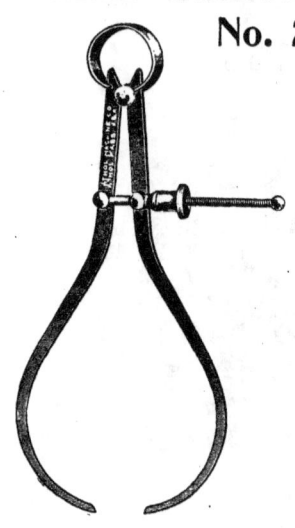

PRICES

	With Quick Nut	With Solid Nut
2½ in.	$0.80	$0.65
3 "	.85	.70
4 "	.90	.75
5 "	.95	.80
6 "	1.00	.85
8 "	1.15	1.00

Premier Inside Spring Calipers No. 220

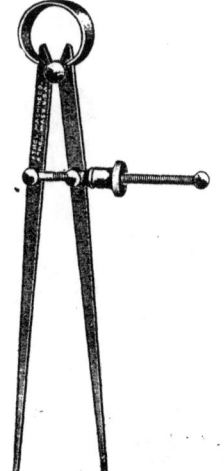

PRICES

	With Quick Nut	With Solid Nut
2½ in.	$0.80	$0.65
3 "	.85	.70
4 "	.90	.75
5 "	.95	.80
6 "	1.00	.85
8 "	1.15	1.00

ATHOL MACHINE CO.   ATHOL, MASS. U.S.A.

Premier Spring Dividers
No. 240

Tempered

PRICES

	With Quick Nut	With Solid Nut
2½ in.	$0.80	$0.65
3 "	.85	.70
4 "	.90	.75
5 "	.95	.80
6 "	1.00	.85
8 "	1.25	1.10

Premier Thread Spring Calipers

Depth of Thread

No. 266

PRICES

	With Quick Nut	With Solid Nut
3 in.	$0.85	$0.70
4 "	.90	.75
5 "	.95	.80

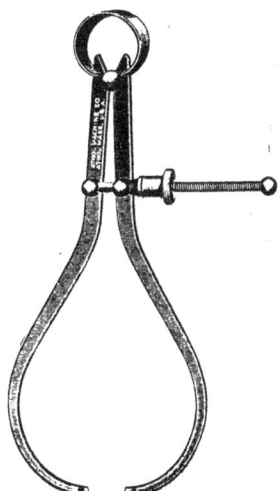

ATHOL MACHINE CO.   ATHOL, MASS. U.S.A.

272
280

Premier Inside Thread Spring Calipers

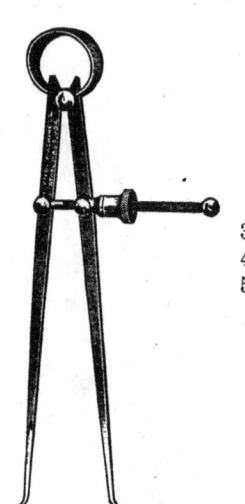

No. 272

PRICES

	With Quick Nut	With Solid Nut
3 in.	$0.85	$0.70
4 "	.90	.75
5 "	.95	.80

Premier Keyhole Spring Calipers

No. 280

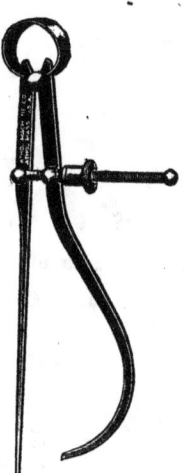

PRICES

	With Quick Nut	With Solid Nut
3 in.	$0.85	$0.70
4 "	.90	.75

Premier Straight Leg Spring Calipers

No. 284

PRICES

	With Quick Nut	With Solid Nut
3 in.	$0.85	$0.70
4 "	.90	.75

Premier Hermaphrodite Spring Calipers
No. 290

PRICES

	With Quick Nut	With Solid Nut
3 in.	$0.85	$0.70
4 "	.90	.75
5 "	.95	.80
6 "	1.00	.85

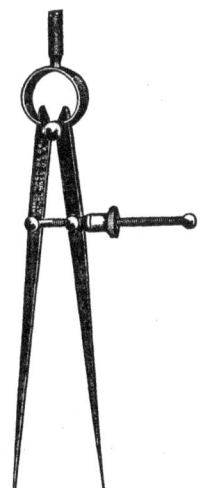

A. M. C. Outside Spring Calipers
No. 300

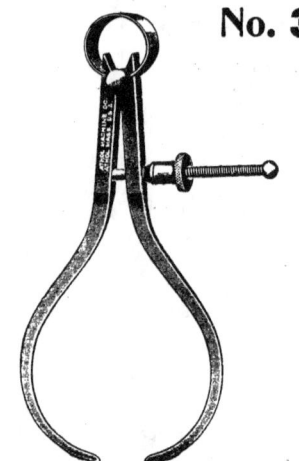

PRICES

	With Quick Nut	With Solid Nut
2½ in.	$1.15	$1.00
3 "	1.15	1.00
4 "	1.25	1.10
5 "	1.25	1.10
6 "	1.50	1.35
8 "	1.75	1.60

A. M. C. Inside Spring Calipers
No. 320

PRICES

	With Quick Nut	With Solid Nut
2½ in.	$1.15	$1.00
3 "	1.15	1.00
4 "	1.25	1.10
5 "	1.25	1.10
6 "	1.50	1.35
8 "	1.75	1.60

ATHOL MACHINE CO.   ATHOL, MASS. U.S.A.

340
360

A. M. C. Spring Dividers
Tempered
No. 340

PRICES

	With Quick Nut	With Solid Nut
2½ in.	$1.15	$1.00
3 "	1.15	1.00
4 "	1.40	1.25
5 "	1.40	1.25
6 "	1.75	1.60
8 "	2.00	1.85

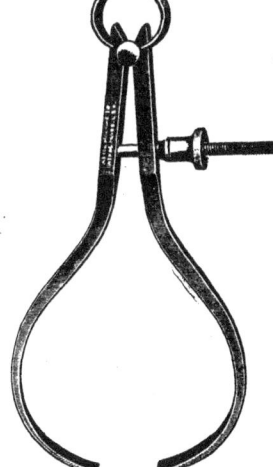

A. M. C. Thread Spring Calipers
No. 360

PRICES

	With Quick Nut	With Solid Nut
3 in.	$1.15	$1.00
4 "	1.25	1.10
5 "	1.25	1.10

ATHOL MACHINE CO.   ATHOL, MASS. U.S.A.

A. M. C. Keyhole Spring Calipers

No. 368

PRICES

	With Quick Nut	With Solid Nut
3 in.	$1.15	$1.00
4 "	1.25	1.10

Parts of Premier Calipers and Dividers

PRICES

Leg $0.25	Screw and Ball.......$0.15
Spring .... .25	Thumb Piece .... .15
Solid Nut............. .10	Fulcrum Stud......... .10
Spring Nut........... .25	Jam Washer.......... .10

Parts of A. M. C. Calipers and Dividers

PRICES

Leg $0.35	Screw and Ball $0.15
Spring .... .25	Thumb Piece......... .15
Solid Nut............. .10	Fulcrum Stud......... .10
Spring Nut........... .25	Jam Washer.......... .10

ATHOL MACHINE CO.   ATHOL, MASS. U.S.A.

530
531

Firm Joint Inside Calipers

Tempered

No. 530

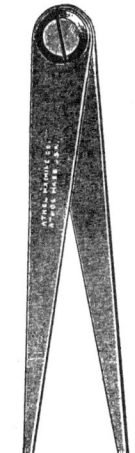

PRICES

4 in....	....	$0.50
5 "	....	.55
6 "	....	.65
8 "	....	.80
10 "	....	.90
12 "	....	1.00
14 "	....	1.50

Firm Joint Outside Calipers

Tempered
No. 531

PRICES

4 in	....	$0.50
5 "	....	.55
6 "	....	.65
8 "	....	.80
10 "	....	.90
12 "	....	1.00
14 "	....	1.50

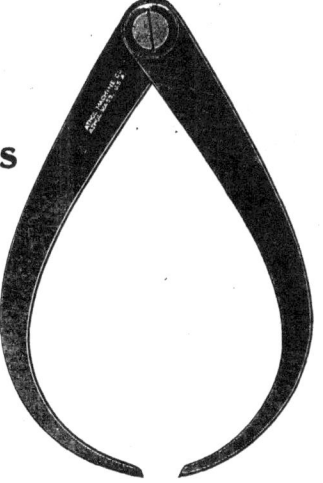

560
561

ATHOL MACHINE CO.   ATHOL, MASS. U.S.A.

Firm Joint Hermaphrodite Calipers

Tempered

No. 560

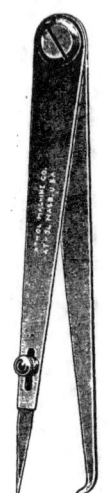

PRICES

4 in.	$0.65
6 "	.80
8 "	1.00
10 "	1.20

Firm Joint Hermaphrodite Calipers

Tempered
With Bent Leg

No. 561

PRICES

4 in.	$0.65
6 "	.80
8 "	1.00
10 "	1.20

Extension Dividers No. 552

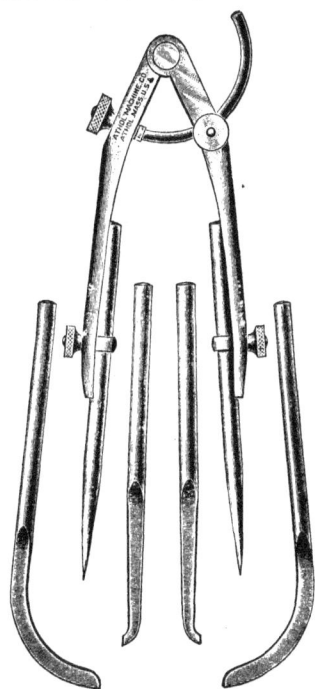

Steel Points Tempered
Sent complete unless otherwise ordered

Size	Circle Scribed	Caliper Capacity	
		Outside	Inside
6 in.	32 in.	14 in.	16 in.
8 "	41 "	18 "	20 "
10 "	50 "	24 "	26 "

PRICES

6 in. with Divider Legs only $1.25	6 in. Complete	$2.25
8 in. " " " " 1.50	8 in. "	2.50
10 in. " " " " 1.75	10 in. "	2.75

ATHOL MACHINE CO.   ATHOL, MASS. U.S.A.

563

Extension Dividers

No. **563**

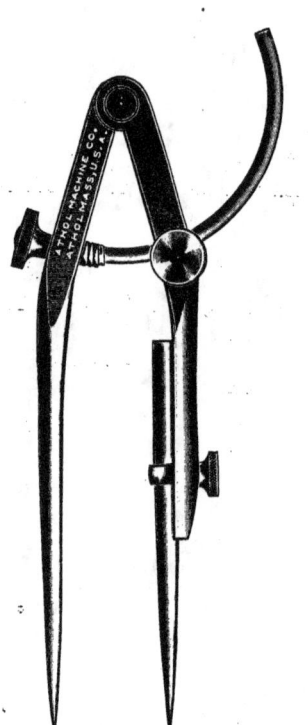

This cut shows our new dividers, with one drop forged leg and one malleable leg, with tool steel points nicely tempered, and an adjustable point which may be instantly removed and a pencil inserted in its place. This tool is light, yet strong, accurately adjusted, and is the best of its class on the market.

PRICES

6 in.	. .	$0.85
8 "	. .	1.00
10 "	. .	1.25

ATHOL MACHINE CO.　　　ATHOL, MASS. U.S.A.

Standard Steel Rules

No. 512

Spring Tempered

Specify length and style of graduation wanted.

Rules of No. 4 graduation will be sent unless otherwise ordered.

No. 1 Graduation		No. 2 Graduation	
1st corner	10, 20, 50, 100	1st corner	10, 20, 50, 100
2d "	12, 24, 48	2d "	12, 24, 48
3d "	16, 32, 64	3d "	16, 32, 64
4th "	14, 28	4th "	8

No. 4 Graduation		No. 7 Graduation	
1st corner	64	1st corner	64
2d "	32	2d "	32
3d "	16	3d "	16
4th "	8	4th "	100

PRICES

1 in	$0.15	12 in	$1.25
2 "	.25	18 "	2.00
3 "	.35	24 "	2.50
4 "	.45	36 "	5.50
6 "	.65	48 "	7.00
9 "	1.00		

ATHOL MACHINE CO.   ATHOL, MASS. U.S.A.

513
514

Steel Straight Edges

No. 513

Not graduated

PRICES

12 in. long,	1	in. wide,	$\frac{3}{16}$	in. thick		....	$	1.20
18 " "	$1\frac{1}{4}$	" "	$\frac{3}{16}$	"	"	....		1.80
24 " "	$1\frac{1}{2}$	" "	$\frac{3}{16}$	"	"	....		2.40
36 " "	2	" "	$\frac{1}{4}$	"	"	....		5.00
48 " "	$2\frac{1}{2}$	" "	$\frac{1}{4}$	"	"	....		8.00
60 " "	3	" "	$\frac{1}{4}$	"	"	....		12.00
72 " "	3	" "	$\frac{1}{4}$	"	"	....		16.00

Beveled Steel Straight Edges

No. 514

Not graduated

The beveled edges are $\frac{1}{16}$ in. thick. Only one edge is beveled.

PRICES

12 in. long,	1 in. wide,	$\frac{3}{16}$ in. thick	.... $1.50
18 " "	$1\frac{1}{4}$ " "	$\frac{3}{16}$ " "	.... 2.50
24 " "	$1\frac{1}{2}$ " "	$\frac{3}{16}$ " "	.... 3.50
36 " "	2 " "	$\frac{1}{4}$ " "	.... 6.00

ATHOL MACHINE CO.   ATHOL, MASS. U.S.A.

500

Combination Square
No. **500**

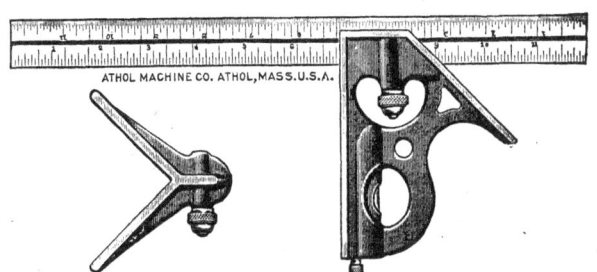

A set complete comprises a Miter Head, Center Head and Blade, as shown in above cut, one blade fitting both heads.

The Set Complete will be sent in all cases unless otherwise specially ordered.

PRICES

	Set Complete		Without Center Head
No. 500 A, 6 in.	$1.50	No. 500 B,	$1.00
No. 500 C, 9 "	1.75	No. 500 D,	1.25
No. 500 E, 12 "	2.00	No. 500 F,	1.50

PRICES OF SEPARATE PARTS

	Blade	Miter Head	Center Head
6 in.	$0.75	$0.50	$0.50
9 "	1.00	.50	.50
12 "	1.25	.75	.50

ATHOL MACHINE CO.   ATHOL, MASS. U.S.A.

501
502

Graduated Steel Square
No. **501**

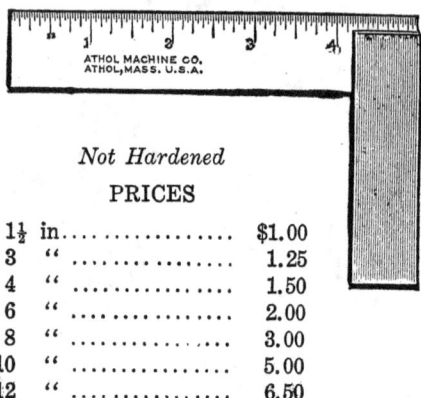

Not Hardened

PRICES

1½ in	....	$1.00
3 "	....	1.25
4 "	....	1.50
6 "	....	2.00
8 "	....	3.00
10 "	....	5.00
12 "	....	6.50

Hardened Steel Square
No. **502**

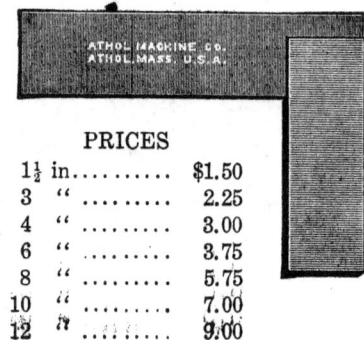

PRICES

1½ in	....	$1.50
3 "	....	2.25
4 "	....	3.00
6 "	....	3.75
8 "	....	5.75
10 "	....	7.00
12 "	....	9.00

ATHOL MACHINE CO. ATHOL, MASS. U.S.A.

503
568

Universal Bevel
No. **503**

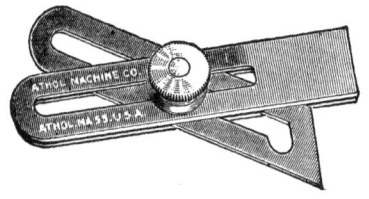

PRICES

Length	Width	
3 in.	⅝ in.	$1.25
5 "	¾ "	2.00

Universal Bevel
No. **568**

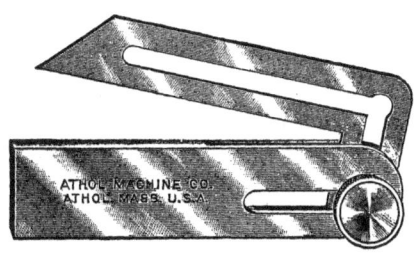

PRICES

Length	Width	
3 in.	⅝ in.	$1.50
5 "	¾ "	2.25

Graduated Depth Gauge
No. 507

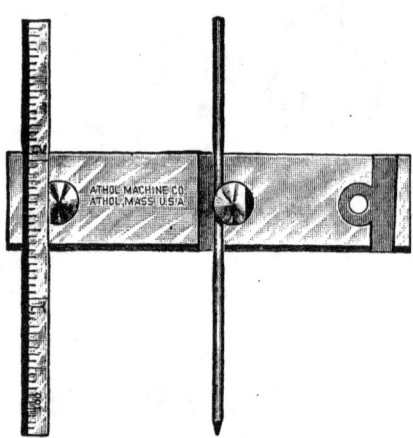

This gauge is provided with a blade, three inches long and three sixteenths of an inch wide, graduated on one side in 64ths and on the other in 100ths, drawn to its seat with a screw having a head with a beveled edge, and locked with a thumb nut on reverse side. Both edges of the beam and the blade are accurately ground.

A wire is also sent with the gauge for use in holes too small to admit the blade and is held by a groove under the round edge of screw head.

The third slot is cut at an angle of one degree for use in die work, and for getting the draft on patterns.

Price $1.25

ATHOL MACHINE CO.   ATHOL, MASS. U.S.A.

509
Graduated Center Gauge
536
537

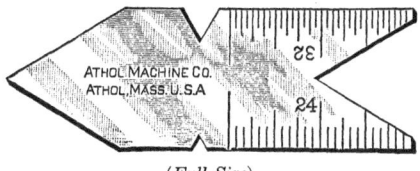

(*Full Size*)

Angle 60 degrees. Graduated in sixteenths, twentieths, twenty-fourths, and thirty-seconds.

PRICES

No. 536.	Not tempered	.	.	. $0.25
No. 537.	Spring tempered	.	.	. .35

Combination Pliers
No. 509

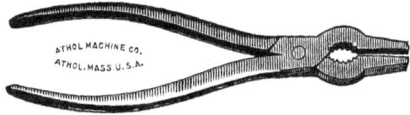

The utility of this tool will be seen at a glance. It is a combination of the common flat plier and a gas plier, and is made from the best hardened tool steel.

PRICES

5 in.	.	.	.	.	.	.	. $0.60
6 "	.	.	.	.	.	.	. .70
7 "	.	.	.	.	.	.	. .75

ATHOL MACHINE CO.   ATHOL, MASS. U.S.A.

566
567

Key Ring Screw Pitch Gauge
No. **566**

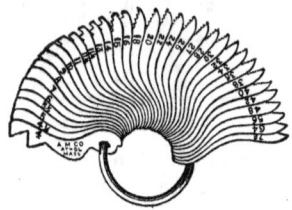

34 Pitches, 4 to 72

CAN BE USED INSIDE OR OUTSIDE
Price, 75 cents

Premier Screw Pitch Gauge
No. **567**

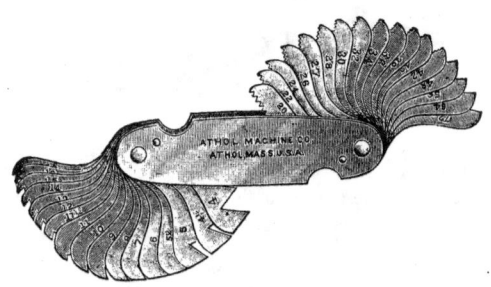

FOR INSIDE AND OUTSIDE WORK
A full line of pitches as shown in cut from 4 to 72
Price, $1.25

ATHOL MACHINE CO.   ATHOL, MASS. U.S.A.

555
564

Drill Blocks No. 555

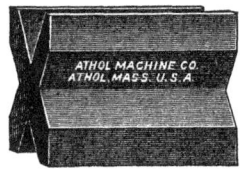 

Furnished in pairs. Size each, 2 in. x 1½ in.
PRICE
Per pair............................$1.00

Drill Block Clamps No. 564

This cut shows the clamp as used in connection with No. 555 Drill Blocks. It holds the round piece up to 1⅛ in. diameter firmly in the groove for prick punching, drilling, or laying out a series of holes before and while being drilled.

Price, $0.50

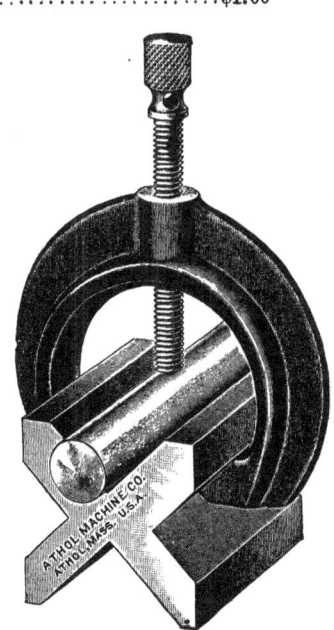

ATHOL MACHINE CO.   ATHOL, MASS. U.S.A.

The Boss Hand Vise No. 540

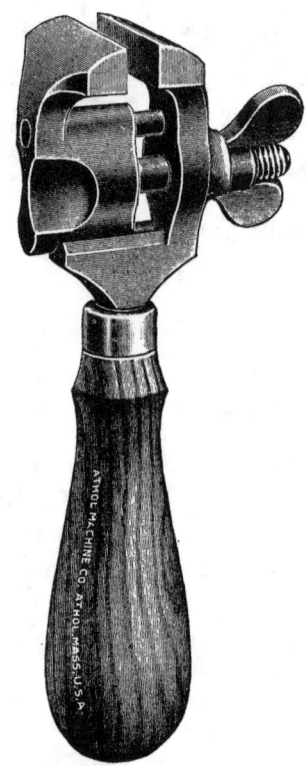

This vise (except handle) is hardened throughout and finely finished with polished jaws.

	Width of Jaws	Jaws open	Weight	Price
No. 540 A	1¼ in.	¾ in.	1-2 lb.	$0.75
No. 540 B	1½ "	1 "	3-4 "	1.00

Standard Hand Vise
No. 549

(Cut Half Size)

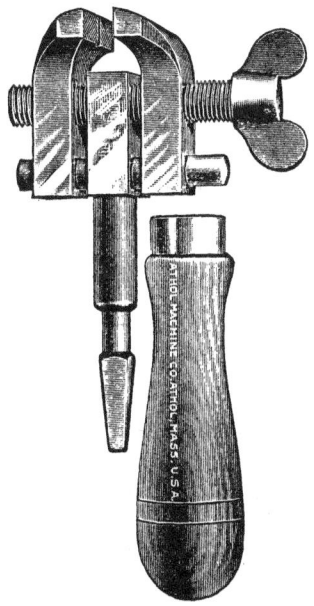

Drop forged and tempered steel jaws, finished either black or bright; the handles on bright finished vises being of cocobolo, and on the black vises of cherry.

A first-class tool in every respect.

Width of Jaws	Jaws open	Weight	Black	Bright
			\multicolumn{2}{c}{PRICES}	
No. 549 A 1¼ in.	1¼ in.	14 ozs.	$1.25	$1.50
No. 549 B 1½ "	1½ "	18 "	1.50	1.75

ATHOL MACHINE CO. ATHOL, MASS. U.S.A.

541

Rapid Transit Wrench

In offering to the trade the tool shown on the opposite page, it is our intention to supply the demand for a well-made and durable wrench. This bar is of open-hearth steel, drop-forged and case-hardened. The screw lies flat on the bar, which prevents its being bent or sprung, and a spring under the point on which the thumb rests (see cut) draws the nut to a true bearing, and takes up all wear. The sliding jaw and the working parts are of steel, all hardened and nicely fitted, thus insuring a strong and durable tool.

The method of operating is so clearly shown in the cut that a description seems almost needless. A slight pressure of the thumb disengages the nut from the screw, permitting the jaw to be moved rapidly the full length of the bar, and as soon as the pressure is removed the nut instantly resumes its place, and the screw can be used to tighten the grip if necessary. We believe it to be the best wrench on the market, and one that every workman will appreciate.

ATHOL MACHINE CO.   ATHOL, MASS. U.S.A.

Rapid Transit Wrench No. **541**

For use on Automobiles, Motor Boats, and by Mechanics generally.

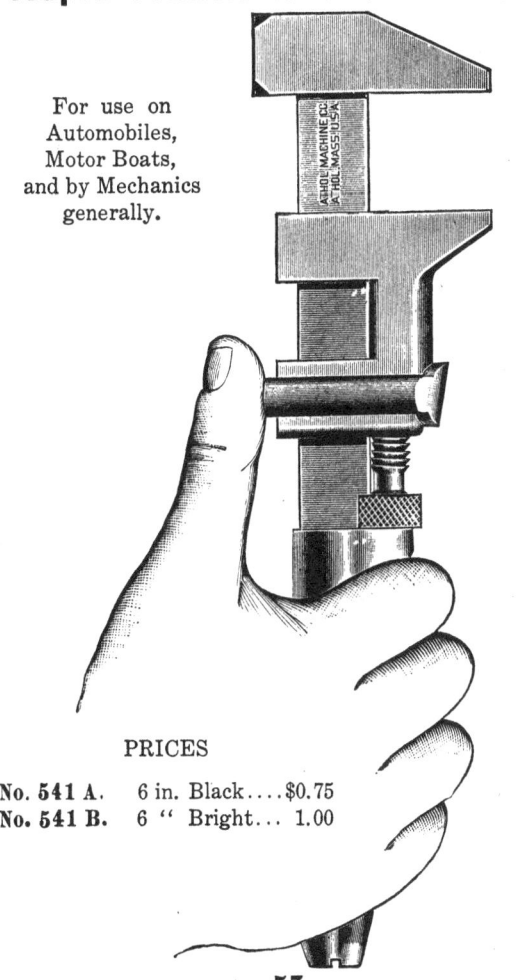

PRICES

No. 541 A. 6 in. Black....$0.75
No. 541 B. 6 " Bright... 1.00

ATHOL MACHINE CO.   ATHOL, MASS. U.S.A.

Machinists' Clamp

No. 544

Strong enough for rough usage.

Made from steel, case-hardened and ground true. Hardened screws.

Prices are for single clamps.

PRICES

Size	Jaws Open	Each
2 in.	1½ in.	$0.75
3 "	2½ "	1.00
4 "	3 "	1.25
5 "	3½ "	1.50
6 "	5¼ "	1.75

Tool Makers' Parallel Clamps

No. 557

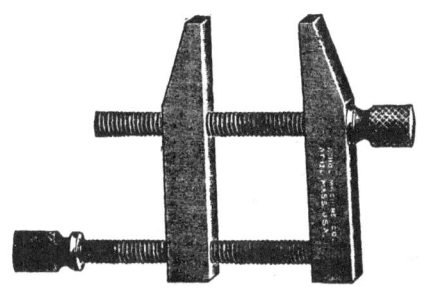

Prices are for single clamps

PRICES

Size	Jaws open	Each
$1\frac{1}{2}$ in.	1 in.	$0.50
2 "	$1\frac{1}{4}$ "	.65
$2\frac{1}{2}$ "	$1\frac{3}{4}$ "	.75
3 "	$2\frac{1}{4}$ "	.85

ATHOL MACHINE CO. ATHOL, MASS. U.S.A.

Carpenters' and Machinists' Iron Levels

With Double Plumb

No. 435

PRICES

4 in.	each,	$1.35
6 "	"	1.50
9 "	"	1.65
12 "	"	1.75
18 "	"	2.00
24 "	"	2.25

With adjustable vial in level, any size, extra, $0.50

The 4 in. has level vial only; the other sizes have double plumbs.

Base of levels grooved for cylindrical work. The groove is exactly parallel with the edge of the base.

These levels are of handsome design, accurate, and surpassed by no others on the market.

ATHOL MACHINE CO.   ATHOL, MASS. U.S.A.

Iron Pocket Level No. 436

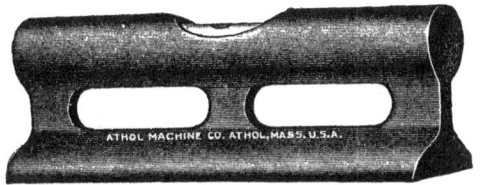

Warranted accurate

PRICES

2¼ in.	$0.25
3½ "	.30

Grooved Level No. 438

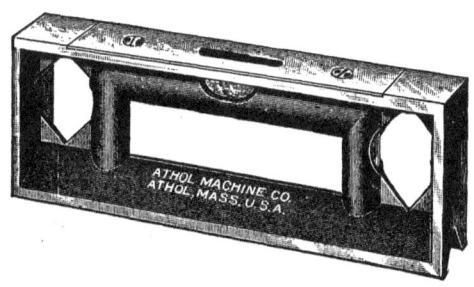

PRICES

6 in., $1.50   9 in., $1.65   12 in., $1.75

ATHOL MACHINE CO.   ATHOL, MASS. U.S.A.

Patent Shafting and Plumbers' Level

No. 439

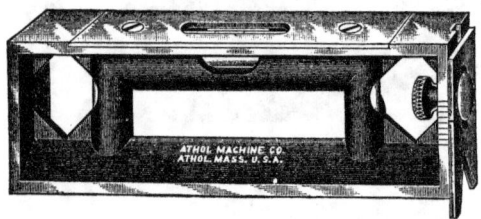

This level is grooved on the bottom the whole length, which any one who has occasion to level up shafting, piping, etc., will see the advantage of, as it enables the user to place the level in line with the shaft or pipe as readily as on a flat surface. These levels are so made that they can be used on a flat surface the same as ordinary levels.

The Plumbers' Level has also a graduated plate on one end that can be adjusted to give the exact pitch of pipes, etc.

PRICES

6 in. . . $2.00   12 in. . . $2.25

Nickel Plated Pocket Levels

No. 442

PRICES

2½ in. . . $0.40   3½ in. . . $0.50

Leveling Instrument
No. 441

Warranted to be true in every respect.

The best, the cheapest, and most durable in the market for the money.

It is adapted for the use of architects, carpenters, builders, stone masons, and others, for leveling, getting angles, etc.

It is made of iron, japanned, except the sight tube, which is of brass, nickel plated. It weighs, when packed in box for shipment, 13¾ pounds. Directions sent with instrument.

PRICES

No. 441 A. Japanned, nickeled tube . . . $12.50
No. 441 B. Japanned, nickeled tube, with ground
            vial in level 14.00

ATHOL MACHINE CO. ATHOL, MASS. U.S.A.

Transit

No. 440

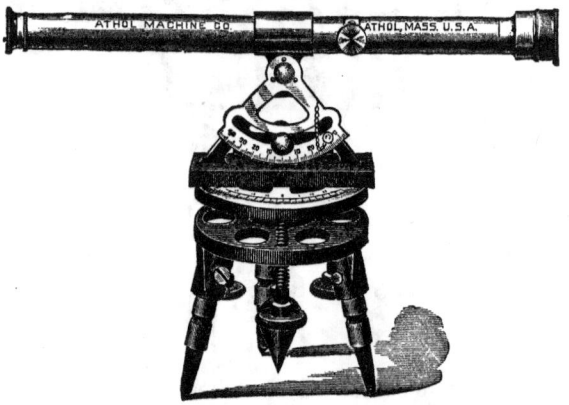

This instrument consists of a tripod, to the head of which is connected an upper plate carrying a graduated arc and a level with plain sight tube.

It is designed for architects, carpenters, and contractors, to lay out building sites and determine the levels; for masons and millwrights in the construction of foundations and the setting of water wheels; building of dams and raceways. The farmer will find it convenient to ascertain the amount of fall for the location of drains, or to find the height of springs; and, when the bearing of lines is not required, the surveyor will find this superior to the ordinary needle compass, for angles may be taken where, from local attraction, it would not be possible to set them off with the needle.

It will be especially appreciated by all who need a level and some instrument for the taking of angles, but do not care to pay the price usually charged for a surveyor's or engineer's transit.

ATHOL MACHINE CO.   ATHOL, MASS. U.S.A.

440

Transit

No. 440—Continued

The instrument is composed of iron and brass, and consists of a tripod, to the head of which is connected by a ball-and-socket joint an upper plate, which can be leveled by the leveling screws.

This plate is recessed to contain a graduated arc for taking angles. On this plate rests a triangular frame to which are attached a level, a graduated arc for taking vertical angles, and a sight tube. The plain sight tube has no lenses, is brass, twelve inches long; in one end is a small eye aperture, in the other the usual cross wires.

The telescope has cross lines, is adjustable to distances, and is same size and length as plain sight tube.

With short legs, as shown in the cut, the instrument is eight inches high. With long extension legs, which fasten on over the short, the height can be from two feet eight inches to four feet eight inches. The sight tube, level case, and graduated arcs are nickel plated, the other parts are japanned.

The advantages of this transit are as follows: The head is held to the tripod with a bolt and nut, so as to make it stationary at any given point; the graduated arc can be clamped to the base-plate by throwing a small cam arrangement.

All points taken into consideration, this transit is one of the best of its kind in the market. It is adapted to almost all kinds of work, is made of the best of materials, and finished and adjusted by skilled workmen. It is warranted perfect and accurate in every respect.

When packed and ready for shipment it weighs about 15 pounds.

Directions for setting up and using are inclosed with each transit, and will be mailed on request to any one interested.

No. 440 F will be sent when style is not specified.

PRICES

No. 440 A	With plain sight tube and short legs	$15.00
No. 440 B	With plain sight tube and long legs	16.50
No. 440 C	With plain sight tube, short legs, and ground level vial	16.50
No. 440 D	With plain sight tube, long legs, and ground level vial	18.00
No. 440 E	With telescope, short legs, and ground level vial	26.50
No. 440 F	With telescope, long legs, and ground level vial	28.00

Target to go on common ten-foot pole, extra $1.50

ATHOL MACHINE CO.   ATHOL, MASS. U.S.A.

Domestic Press No. 400

For the use of families, hotels, and restaurants in pressing corned beef, boiled mutton, tongue, boned turkey, headcheese, and other meats, and in extracting the juice from fruit and berries; for making domestic wines, grape and currant jellies, etc.; also for pressing lard, cottage cheese, squash, turnip, and other vegetables.

Corned beef, tongue, boiled chicken, and all meats designed to be eaten cold, are greatly improved by being pressed, as a single trial will demonstrate. The meat should be placed in the press while hot, the fat and lean in layers, and be allowed to remain under pressure until thoroughly cooled. Meats thus treated retain their juices, have a more delicate flavor, and, when wanted for the table, can be served in a style otherwise quite impossible.

PRICES

No. 400 A.	Size, 6 x 9 and 4 in. deep,	$2.50
No. 400 B.	Size, 8 x 12 and 5 " "	3.50
No. 400 C.	Size, 10 x 14 and 6 " "	4.50

PRICES OF PARTS

	No. 400 A	No. 400 B	No. 400 C
Yoke	$0.33	$0.42	$0.50
Screw	.25	.35	.40
Follower	.40	.60	.80
Perforated Tin	.25	.33	.40
Base and Rim	1.50	2.00	2.50

ATHOL MACHINE CO.   ATHOL, MASS. U.S.A.

Improved American Meat and Vegetable Chopper

For cutting Sausage Meat, Mince Meat, Salads, Hash, Fish, Fruit, Vegetables, Etc.

This is the only Family Meat Cutter made that *chops* the food precisely as it is chopped by hand, with the old chopping knife and tray, leaving it coarse or fine as may best suit the taste.

It is extremely simple in construction, and does its work with such ease and rapidity that a child six years of age can chop in four minutes as much as can be cut in an hour with the old chopping knife and tray.

These choppers do not *grind* or *tear* the meat, leaving it in strings, like the grinders in common use, nor do they *mash* the food like those machines, *miscalled choppers*, which work with a shearing cut under pressure, leaving it a pasty mass, but every particle of the material is *chopped* and is left dry and light, and more evenly and thoroughly mixed than is possible with any other machine.

Should be in Every Household

As a family machine for chopping cooked meats, vegetables, fruit, etc., for making mince pies, salads, corned beef or vegetable hash, fish balls, headcheese, and the like, these choppers are not only far ahead of all other devices for that purpose, but are absolutely the only ones yet invented that will do the work in a satisfactory and expeditious manner.

In all other cutters more or less of the material to be chopped adheres to the knives and other parts of the machine, not only causing a loss of food, but the annoyance and difficulty of cleaning is so great as to make them of little or no value in preparing small quantities of food, while the American is equally useful, whether a large or small quantity is required, there being but two pieces to clean, the knife and the dish, both of which are readily removed for the purpose, and are as easily and as quickly cleaned as a common chopping knife and bowl.

These choppers are largely used by druggists and apothecaries in making tinctures, extracts, etc., and are recommended by leading physicians everywhere for preparing food for invalids.

They are the best machines in the market for chopping food for fowls, and are extensively used by poultry fanciers and breeders throughout the country.

They are also in use by all the principal fish breeders and proprietors of trout ponds in the country, and are the only machines with which food for the young fry can be properly prepared.

ATHOL MACHINE CO. ATHOL, MASS. U.S.A.

401
402

American Meat Chopper

Family Sizes

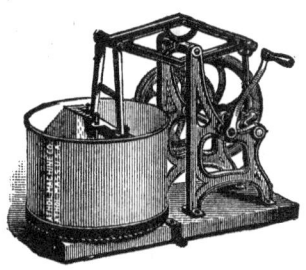

No family, however small, should be without one, while for hotels, restaurants, and public institutions where large quantities of food are required, they are absolutely indispensable.

The principal working parts are made of the best malleable iron, rendering a breakage impossible by any ordinary or reasonable usage.

No. **401**

	Cuts 3 lbs. in three minutes	
8-in. Cylinder.	Weight, 14 lbs.	Price $5.00

No. **402**

	Cuts 5 to 6 lbs. in three minutes	
10-in. Cylinder.	Weight, 21 lbs.	Price $7.00

ATHOL MACHINE CO.   ATHOL, MASS. U.S.A.

403
404

American Meat Chopper
Hotel Sizes

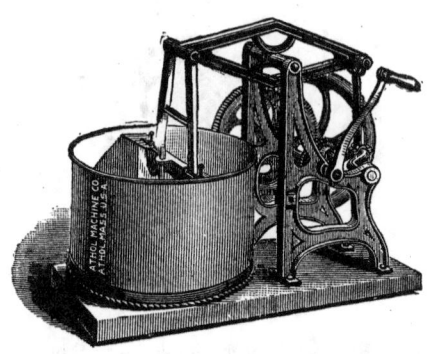

These sizes are made very strong and heavy, and are special favorites with farmers for cutting sausage meat, as well as for large hotels and restaurants.

The No. 404 is the same size as the No. 403, but has an intermittent gear feed like the butchers' sizes, instead of a ratchet and pawl like the family sizes.

No. 403

Cuts 8 to 10 lbs. in three to four minutes
12-in. Cylinder.   Weight, 37 lbs.   Price $10.00

No. 404

Cuts 8 to 10 lbs. in three to four minutes
12-in. Cylinder   Weight, 43 lbs.   Price $12.00

ATHOL MACHINE CO.   ATHOL, MASS. U.S.A.

405
406
407

American Meat Chopper

Butchers' Sizes

These choppers are too well known to need either an extended description or recommendation. They are pronounced by butchers who have had them in constant use for years—"THE BEST SAUSAGE CUTTERS IN AMERICA."

No. 405 is specially adapted for the use of small butchers and marketmen, and for their work it has no equal in market. This size is also extensively used in public institutions, schools, hospitals, etc.

No. 406 is in all respects similar to the No. 407 shown in the cut, with the exception that it has but one crank, and the cylinder is two inches smaller in diameter.

No. 407 has two cranks, as shown in the cut, and can be easily operated by two boys; or, by putting a pulley in place of the main crank, it can be arranged to run by power, at a trifling expense.

ATHOL MACHINE CO. ATHOL, MASS. U.S.A.

405

American Meat Chopper

Butchers' Sizes

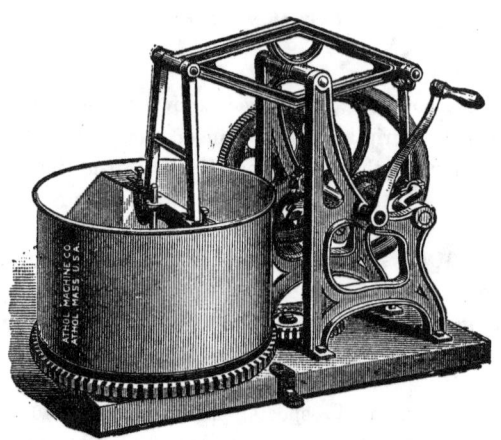

No. 405

Butchers and marketmen get from 1 to 3 cts. per lb. more for sausage cut with one of these choppers than when cut, or mashed, with the "Grinders" so commonly used.

Cuts from 50 to 60 lbs. an hour
Weight, crated ready for shipment, 120 lbs.
15-in. Block.   Price $25.00

ATHOL MACHINE CO.   ATHOL, MASS. U.S.A.

American Meat Chopper
Butchers' Sizes

406
407

No. 406

With one crank, cuts from 60 to 80 lbs. an hour
Weight, crated ready for shipment, 275 lbs.
18-in. Block.   Price $50.00

No. 407

Cuts from 80 to 100 lbs. an hour
Weight, crated ready for shipment, 300 lbs.
20-in. Block.   Price $60.00
Tight and Loose Pulley for power, $8.00

ATHOL MACHINE CO. ATHOL, MASS. U.S.A.

American Meat Chopper

Extra Parts

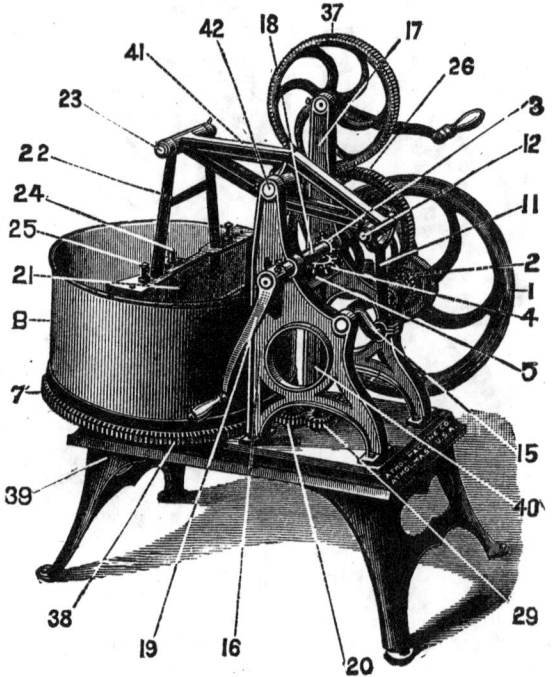

For Price List of Extra Parts, as shown above, see next page. Corresponding parts bear the same number in each size of machine.

ATHOL MACHINE CO. ATHOL, MASS. U.S.A.

Price List of Extra Parts

No.	American Meat and Veg. Chopper	401	402	403 404	405	406	407
1	Balance Wheel	$0.50	$0.70	$1.00	$1.90	$3.00	$3.50
2	Balance Wheel Gear	....	....	....	....	.90	.90
3	Bevel Pinion, on Gear Shaft	....	....	.17	.25	.40	.40
4	Bevel Gear, on Upright Shaft	....	....	.20	.25	.40	.40
5	Brace, for Upright Shaft	....	....	.22	.30	.50	.50
6	Cylinder, complete	.80	1.10	1.85	5.75	9.00	10.50
7	Cylinder Plate, Iron	.30	.40	1.00	1.60	2.50	2.75
8	Cylinder Rim, Tin or Galv. Iron	.35	.45	.60	1.50	2.00	2.25
9	Cylinder Wood, with Hub	.25	.30	.37	2.75	4.00	5.25
10	Cylinder Hub	.06	.08	.10	.15	.40	.40
11	Connecting Rod	.25	.35	.50	.75	1.25	1.25
12	Connecting Rod Pin	.12	.15	.17	.20	.30	.30
13	Collar for Upright Shaft	....	....	.12	.15	.20	.20
14	Clamp	.15	.15	.18	.10	....	....
15	Crank Shaft	.30	.40	.50	.75	1.25	1.25
16	Frame Piece, Handle Side	.37	.50	.65	1.50	2.75	2.75
17	Frame Piece, Balance Wheel Side	.37	.50	.65	1.50	2.75	3.25
18	Gear Shaft	.20	.25	.35	.60	1.00	1.00
19	Handle	.25	.30	.40	.60	.85	.85
20	Intermediate Gear	....	....	.20	.25	.35	.30
21	Knife	.50	.65	.85	1.35	3.00	3.50
22	Knife Frame	.45	.60	.80	1.30	2.00	2.50
23	Knife Frame Pin	.15	.17	.20	.25	.40	.40
24	Knife Guide Rod	.20	.25	.40	.60	.80	.80
25	Knife Set Screw	.03	.04	.04	.10	.12	.12
26	Large Gear	.15	.20	.40	.50	1.00	1.00
27	Pawl	.15	.18	.25	....	....	1.00
28	Pawl Guide, with Spring	.15	.17	.20	....	....	1.00
29	Pinion, on Upright Shaft	....	....	.20	.25	.30	.30
30	Pulley	....	....	....	....	....	2.75
31	Step, for Upright Shaft	....	....	.30	.35	....	....
32	Small Screws, two cents each	....	....	....	....	....	....
33	Set Screws and Pawl Screws	.05	.06	.08	.06	.08	.08
34	Spiral Springs	....	....	.05	.05	.08	.08
35	Split Pins	....	....	....	....	.03	.03
36	Tap Bolts and Table Bolts	.03	.03	.04	.06	.08	.08
37	Top Gear, with Handle	....	....	....	....	....	2.00
38	Table or Stand, complete	.35	.50	.65	1.50	12.50	12.50
39	Table or Stand Leg	....	....	....	....	2.00	2.00
40	Upright Shaft	....	....	.25	.35	.75	.75
41	Walking Beam	.37	.50	.65	1.50	2.25	2.25
42	Walking Beam Center Pin	.10	.12	.15	.20	.25	.25
43	Wrench	....	....	....	.20	.25	.25

ATHOL MACHINE CO.   ATHOL, MASS. U.S.A.

415

Wright's Animal Tether
No. 415

The cut on the following page shows the uses and advantages of this invention, which is designed to obviate the danger of horses and other animals becoming entangled in the rope with which they are fastened. It consists of a pole about ten feet in length, connected with an upright bar, upon which it turns in any direction. The animal is fastened to the end of this pole by a rope, which is kept taut above his head by means of a spring at the base of the pole; this keeps the pole high in the air, until in reaching for the feed the animal pulls it down, thus at all times keeping the rope from under his feet.

PRICES OF PARTS
Spring	$0.75
Bar Holder	.30
Pole Holder	.25
Rivet	.05
Bar	.75
Rope	.25
Upper Collar	.25
Lower Collar	.15
Pole	.25

Price . . $3.00

ATHOL MACHINE CO.   ATHOL, MASS. U.S.A.

415

Illustrating several uses of Tether No. 415

ATHOL MACHINE CO.   ATHOL, MASS. U.S.A.

Index

Vises, pages 3-25

	PAGE
AMATEUR	15
EXTRA PARTS	23-25
FARMERS'	22
OVAL SLIDE	21
PIPE GRIP	23

SIMPSON

Bench, swivel	7
Bench, stationary	8
Bench, swivel, swivel jaw	10
Bench, stationary, swivel jaw	9
Coachmakers' swivel	12
Coachmakers' stationary	11
Coachmakers' swivel, swivel jaw	14

SIMPSON

Coachmakers' stationary, swivel jaw	13
Jewelers' and Artisans' clamp	6
Jewelers' and Artisans' swivel	6

STANDARD

Bench, swivel	17
Bench, stationary	18
Bench, swivel, swivel jaw	20
Bench, stationary, swivel jaw	19
Jewelers' and Artisans' clamp	16

STANDS 3, 4

Grindstone Frames and Grinders, pages 26-33

BENCH GRINDER No. 158	31	IRON No. 155	27
BENCH GRINDER No. 159	32	IRON No. 156	28
COUNTERSHAFT	33	IRON No. 157	29
HOUSEHOLD	26	TRUER	30

Tools, pages 34-65

BEVELS	49	LEVELING INSTRUMENT	63
CALIPERS AND DIVIDERS	34-44	PLIERS	51
CENTER GAUGES	51	RULES	45
CLAMPS	58, 59	SCREW PITCH GAUGES	52
DEPTH GAUGE	50	SQUARES	47, 48
DIVIDERS AND CALIPERS	34-44	STRAIGHT EDGES	46
DRILL BLOCKS AND CLAMPS	53	TRANSIT	64, 65
HAND VISES	54, 55	WRENCH	56, 57
LEVELS	60-62		

CHOPPERS, MEAT, ETC.	67-73	PRESS, DOMESTIC	66
CHOPPERS, EXTRA PARTS	74, 75	TETHER, ANIMAL	76, 77

ATHOL MACHINE CO.	ATHOL, MASS. U.S.A.

Numerical Index

No.	Page	No.	Page	No.	Page
0	6	81	17	360	39
1	6	82	17	368	40
2	6	83	17	400	66
3	16	87	18	401	69
4	16	88	18	402	69
5	16	89	18	403	70
10	6	90	18	404	70
11	7	91	18	405	72
12	7	92	18	406	73
13	7	93	18	407	73
14	7	94	18	415	76
15	7	95	18	435	60
16	7	96	18	436	61
27	8	101	19	438	61
28	8	102	20	439	62
29	8	103	19	440	64
30	8	104	20	441	63
31	8	105	19	442	62
32	8	106	20	500	47
33	8	107	9	501	48
40	11	108	10	502	48
41	11	109	9	503	49
42	12	110	10	507	50
43	12	111	9	509	51
44	13	112	10	512	45
45	13	150	23	513	46
46	14	154	26	514	46
47	14	155	27	530	41
50	15	156	28	531	41
51	15	157	29	536	51
60	15	158	31	537	51
62	15	159	32	540	54
63	21	160	33	541	57
64	21	161	30	544	58
65	21	200	34	549	55
66	21	220	34	552	43
67	21	240	35	555	53
69	22	266	35	557	59
70	22	272	36	560	42
71	22	280	36	561	42
72	22	284	37	563	44
77	17	290	37	564	53
78	17	300	38	566	52
79	17	320	38	567	52
80	17	340	39	568	49

Athol Vises are Fully Warranted

Our vises are not unbreakable.

We never made one that could not be broken. No one else ever did, either.

They are, however, made of iron and steel best adapted for the purpose. They are so designed that the greatest strength is where the greatest strain comes. Strong where strength is needed. They are carefully made by workmen who know their business, and they are rigidly inspected. Any vise we make will do any work and stand any strain that can reasonably be expected of a vise of its size.

Warranty

We warrant all our vises to be free from defects of material or workmanship. Any vise found defective in either particular will be replaced without charge.

Any vise part which breaks with reasonable usage will be replaced without charge; and we will leave it entirely with the customer to say whether the part broke under reasonable usage or not.

ATHOL MACHINE CO.